D1716593

First
Facts®

UNEXPLAINED MYSTERIES

The Unsolved Mystery of Bigfoot

by Michael Burgan

CAPSTONE PRESS
a capstone imprint

First Facts are published by Capstone Press,
1710 Roe Crest Drive, North Mankato, Minnesota 56003
www.capstonepub.com

Library of Congress Cataloging-in-Publication Data
Burgan, Michael.
 The unsolved mystery of Bigfoot / by Michael Burgan.
   p. cm. — (First facts. Unexplained mysteries.)
 Summary: "Presents the legend of Bigfoot, including current theories and famous encounters"—Provided by publisher.
  ISBN 978-1-62065-134-6 (library binding)
  ISBN 978-1-62065-806-2 (paperback)
  ISBN 978-1-4765-1064-4 (eBook PDF)
 1. Sasquatch—Juvenile literature. I. Title.
  QL89.2.S2B87 2013
  001.944—dc23   2012028437

Editorial Credits
Mari Bolte, editor; Veronica Correia, designer; Wanda Winch, media researcher,
Jennifer Walker, production specialist

Photo Credits
Corbis: Bettmann, 6, 17; Courtesy of the Agua Caliente Cultural Museum, 9; Fortean Picture Library, 11, 13, 14, 20; Photo taken by Randee Chase up on Silver Star Mountain, Washington, 18; Shutterstock: Andreas Meyer, Bigfoot used throughout book, sgrigor, background; SuperStock Inc: Animals Animals, 4

Printed in China.
092012   006936RRDS13

Table of Contents

This video taken in California shows a creature that looks like a gorilla. But gorillas don't live in California.

A Creature in the Woods

In 1967 two men rode through the mountains of northern California. Suddenly a large hairy creature appeared. The animal was tall and walked on two legs. One of the men filmed the beast as it walked along a stream. Then it disappeared.

Chapter 2

Oregon, California, and Washington are the three top states for Bigfoot sightings.

This picture was taken in northern California in 1981.

History and Legend

People in North America tell stories about an animal that looks like a **primate**. The creature walks on its back legs. It leaves large, humanlike footprints as proof of its existence. But no one has caught this strange creature known as Bigfoot.

primate—any member of the group of intelligent animals that includes humans, apes, and monkeys

American Indians told stories of hairy men living in the woods. Some Canadian tribes called them Sasquatches. This name means "wild men of the woods."

In 1784 a newspaper wrote about Bigfoot in North America. The article told of a large, furry animal. Another newspaper wrote about an apelike creature spotted in 1818.

American Indian cave paintings show creatures that look like Bigfoot.

In the 1850s gold miners saw Bigfoots in California. They said the creatures picked up their tools and smashed them.

A logger named Albert Ostman said a Bigfoot kidnapped him in 1924. The animal took him to where it lived. There he saw three more Bigfoots. One of them was at least 8 feet (2.4 m) tall. He lived with the Bigfoots for six days before escaping.

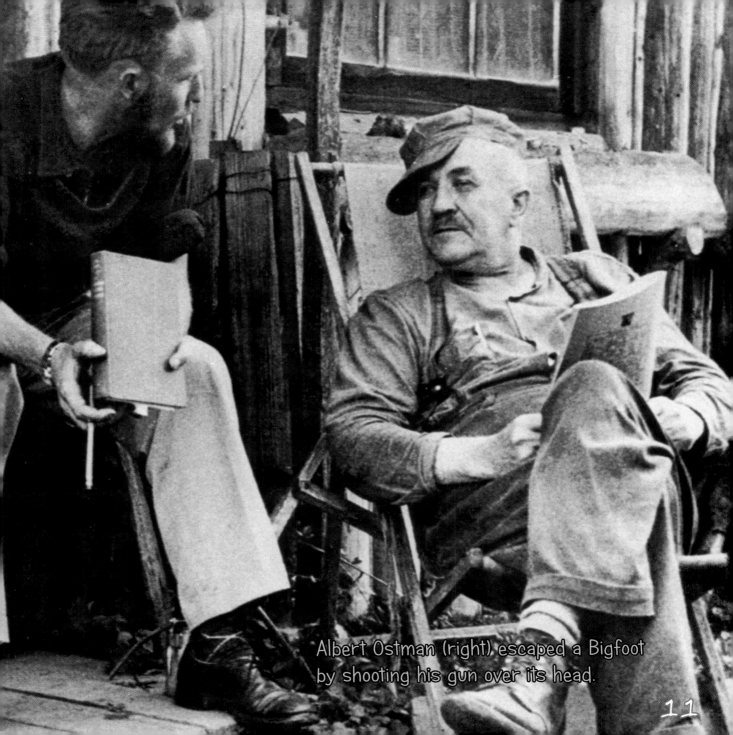

Albert Ostman (right) escaped a Bigfoot
by shooting his gun over its head.

11

Chapter 3

Bigfoot or Not?

People looking for answers about Bigfoots have many ideas. Some people think Bigfoots could be bears. Others say they are **Neanderthals**. They might be large ancient apes called gigantos. Those who don't believe in Bigfoot say the sightings are just people in costumes.

Neanderthal—an early type of human who lived more than 30,000 years ago

13

People collect proof to prove Bigfoot exists. But not all reported Bigfoots look the same. Some pictures show a Bigfoot with wide shoulders and long arms. Others show an animal that looks more like a human covered in dark fur.

Bigfoot footprints have been found with both four and five toes.

True or False?

Can high-tech equipment help researchers find Bigfoot?

True:

- Some Bigfoot hunters wear goggles that help them see in the dark. They believe Bigfoots are most active at night.

- They also use cameras that work best at night.

- In 2012 scientists asked for samples of Bigfoot hair for **DNA** tests.

False:

- Many pictures and videos taken of Bigfoot are blurry.

- Bigfoots live far from humans. This makes them hard to find even with high-tech gear.

- Bigfoot DNA has been tested in the past. Scientists were unable to prove Bigfoot exists.

DNA—material in cells that gives people their individual characteristics

The Bigfoot Field **Researchers** Organization (BFRO) was formed in 1995. The group keeps track of Bigfoot reports. They study footprints, pictures, and videos. They examine clues such as hair and blood that were found near Bigfoot sightings.

researcher—someone who studies a subject to discover new information

Most Bigfoot footprints are at least 14 inches (36 centimeters) long and 6 inches (15 cm) wide.

Chapter 4

Searching for Bigfoot

Bigfoots have been seen around the world. Some people call them yetis or abominable snowmen. These apelike creatures also walk on two legs and are between 6 and 8 feet (1.8 and 2.4 meters) tall.

Some say this photo shows a Bigfoot near Silver Star Mountain in Washington. It was taken in 2005.

True or False?

Is Bigfoot real or just a **myth**?

True:

- Many footprints have been found.

- There are many pictures and videos of Bigfoots.

- People who have seen something strange believe they saw Bigfoot.

False:

- No one has ever caught a Bigfoot.

- No Bigfoot bones have been found.

- Some pictures and video of Bigfoot turned out to be fake.

myth—a false idea that many people believe

People today still report seeing strange, hairy animals in the woods. But no one knows for sure what they are. Until the mystery is solved, people will continue to search for Bigfoot.

Glossary

DNA (dee-en-AY)—material in cells that gives people their individual characteristics

myth (MITH)—a false idea that many people believe

Neanderthal (nee-AN-dur-thal)—an early type of human who lived more than 30,000 years ago

primate (PRYE-mate)—any member of the group of intelligent animals that includes humans, apes, and monkeys

researcher (REE-surch-ur)—someone who studies a subject to discover new information

Read More

McCormick, Lisa Wade. *Bigfoot: The Unsolved Mystery.* Mysteries of Science. Mankato, Minn.: Capstone Press, 2009.

Roberts, Steven. *Bigfoot!* Jr. Graphic Monster Stories. New York: PowerKids Press, 2013.

Theisen, Paul. *Bigfoot.* The Unexplained. Minneapolis: Bellwether Media, 2011.

Internet Sites

FactHound offers a safe, fun way to find Internet sites related to this book. All of the sites on FactHound have been researched by our staff.

Here's all you do:

Visit *www.facthound.com*

Type in this code: 9781620651346

Check out projects, games and lots more at
www.capstonekids.com

23

Index